FRUITFUL AND RESPONSIBLE LOVE

KAROL WOJTYLA
(Pope John Paul II)

FRUITFUL AND RESPONSIBLE LOVE

With contributions by • Giorgio Campanini
Jack Dominian • François and Michele Guy
Vincenzo Lorenzelli • Gustave Martelet
Masamba ma Mpolo • A. F. Mascarenhas
Giacomo Perico • Charles Villa
Max Thurian

A CROSSROAD BOOK
THE SEABURY PRESS • NEW YORK

1979
The Seabury Press
815 Second Avenue
New York, N.Y. 10017

Library of Congress Cataloging in Publication Data

John Paul II, Pope, 1920-
Fruitful and responsible love.
"A Crossroad book."
Delivered as the opening address at the International Congress on
Fruitful and Responsible Love: Ten Years after Humanae Vitae, June
1978. Milan.
1. Love (Theology) — Addresses, essays, lectures. 2. Catholic
Church. Pope, 1963-1978. (Paulus VI) Humanae vitae—Addresses,
essays, lectures. I. Title.
BV4639.J55 1979   261.8'34'26   78-22728   ISBN 0-8164-2237-0

CONTENTS

Foreword

The election of Cardinal Karol Wojtyla to the See of Peter on October 16, 1978, must have aroused many happy memories among the 400 participants from fifty-seven different countries who had attended the international Congress on "Fruitful and Responsible Love: ten years after *Humanae Vitae*". The Congress, held at Milan on June 21-22, was opened by Cardinal Wojtyla, now Pope John Paul II, who spoke on the theme of the meeting.

Cardinal Wojtyla had readily accepted to come from Poland to speak at this Congress, as it gave him "the opportunity to reflect" with the participants "not only on a document of the Church", but "on a pastoral problem which in various ways involves all the people of God". His address was received and discussed with interest throughout the Congress by the delegates, many of whom were non-Catholic and non-Christian. As many observed, the Milan Congress was perhaps one of the few international gatherings of an ecumenical dimension which studied *Humanae Vitae* in an open and scientific manner. The Cardinal's address served as a theological and pastoral foundation for such ecumenical dialogue.

In fact his approach, as can be seen from the text, was deeply concerned with the pastoral aspects of the problem. He admirably analysed the christian concept of love in *Humanae Vitae,* strengthening the thought of Paul VI by several quotations from *The Church in the Modern World (Gaudium et Spes)* (Part II). This was done in a masterly manner, offering much food for thought, for he felt that the pastoral constitution of Vatican II "enlarged the pastoral implications" of the problem. In fact, the encyclical is rendered more relevant when the Pope's words are read in conjunction with those of the College of Bishops, as expressed in the Vatican Council document.

Cardinal Wojtyla's address, translated from Italian, is presented here in full. Since he has now been elected to govern the universal Church, this text acquires a special significance, though it should still be considered as the thoughts of the Archbishop of Cracow.

However, it reflects the interest, concern and reflections of a Pastor who has always had the welfare of the family at heart. Pope Paul VI had appointed him in 1964 a member of the pontifical commission for the study of population, family and birth. He has also written a book on the theme of the Congress. In his own diocese, especially through the deliberations of the Cracow Synod, he has always promoted the family in his pastoral work.

Through this publication the International Centre for the Study of Family Life (C.I.S.F.) — involved as it is in the study, research and promotion of the family — wishes to witness the concern, love and importance which Pope John Paul II has always had for the family. Today, we all look up to him with great expectations for the human and spiritual help to the families throughout the world.

The comments presented along with the text are the reactions of joy and appreciation to Cardinal Wojtyla's address. I am sure they were shared by all the delegates who were with us at Milan.

Fr Charles G. Vella

Fr Charles G. Vella is Director of the Centro Internazionale Studi Famiglia (C.I.S.F.) Milan.

FRUITFUL AND RESPONSIBLE LOVE

Address given by Karol Wojtyla, then Cardinal Archbishop of Cracow, at the international Congress held at Milan in June 1978.

1. *The Tenth Anniversary*

The occasion for this Congress is the tenth anniversary of the appearance of the encyclical *Humanae Vitae,* published by the Holy Father Paul VI on July 25, 1968.

The *Centro Internazionale Studi Famiglia* (C.I.S.F. — International Centre for the Study of Family Life) invites us to reconsider together the key theme of the encyclical: fruitful and responsible love. We are to approach it not only as the theme of a Church document, voicing the teaching of its highest authority, but at the same time as a pastoral problem, in which the whole People of God participates in different ways. This has been clearly stressed in the third and final part of the encyclical *Humanae Vitae,* and at an earlier date also in *Gaudium et Spes,* the pastoral constitution of the Second Vatican Council. The pontifical document has distinctly *developed pastoral indications,* appealing respectively to public authorities and to scientists, addressing those most directly concerned — that is, christian married couples and families — and also those who are, in an indirect way, concerned with responsible parenthood: doctors and all involved in health service, and finally the pastors, priests and bishops of the whole Church in today's world.[1]

To a certain extent our present meeting is also a reply to these various appeals of the Church — of Paul VI, and of the Second Vatican Council. It is an answer given after ten years, and also from the perspective of those ten years themselves, during which there was developing, alongside the various voices of protest and opposition, a methodical effort to show the possibility of respecting divine law in married life, so clearly stressed by Paul VI in *Humanae Vitae* § 20.

What is more, this effort, undertaken on many sides, is in itself an argument taken from a broad range of experience and speaking in favour of the truth of the doctrine contained in the encyclical *Humanae Vitae* and of its essential soundness.

Since this truth and rightness concerns above all the problem of co-ordinating the rhythms of conjugal love and of procreation, it is also appropriate to devote our attention at this Congress chiefly to this subject.

2. *The Encyclical* Humanae Vitae *and the Pastoral Constitution* Gaudium et Spes

To do so it is necessary to turn to the source itself. It is well known that the encyclical is closely connected with the pastoral constitution of Vatican II which, in the first chapter of its

Second Part entitled: *Fostering the Nobility of Marriage and the Family,* treats among others this key subject: *Harmonising Conjugal Love with Respect for Human Life* (GS § 51). We also know that some problems within this field, which demanded deeper analyses and examination under all their aspects, had been handed over to a special Commission (for Problems of Population, Family and Genetics), created back in 1963 by Pope John XXIII, and enlarged by Paul VI in 1964. This Commission was of a purely consultative character; the final judgement upon the matter was to belong to the Pope himself in virtue of his own magisterial authority. That is why we cannot search in the text of the pastoral constitution for concrete solutions, while at the same time it is necessary to refer to its text, since the author of the encyclical did it himself, recalling what had been recently set forth in this regard — and in a highly authoritative form — by the Second Vatican Council in its pastoral constitution *Gaudium et Spes* (HV § 7).

In fact, *the exposition of Gaudium et Spes on the subject of conjugal love* (§ 49) and in turn on the fruitfulness of marriage (§ 50) is even more extensive than that of the encyclical *Humanae Vitae.* It also seems more analytical, while the encyclical treats the subject of conjugal life in a more synthetical way. The pastoral constitution uses a more descriptive method, stressing the christological and sacramental aspect of marriage and enriching the text with many parenthetical injunctions. It contains as it were the whole of christian pedagogy and ethics. The exposition of *Humanae Vitae* is more concise, strictly theological and systematic. It stresses the fact that conjugal love has its "origin" in "God who is Love" and Father; that "by means of the reciprocal gift of self, proper and exclusive to them, husband and wife tend towards the communion of their beings in view of mutual personal perfection, to collaborate with God in the generation and education of new lives" (§ 8).

Paul VI then lists *the characteristics of conjugal love*. "This love is first of all fully human, total, faithful and exclusive, and fruitful". Each of these qualities is concisely described. This love is fully human, and therefore "of the senses and of the spirit at the same time", generated and formed by man and woman not only as a "simple transport of instinct and sentiment", but also and "principally as an act of free will". When defining the totality of conjugal love, the author of *Humanae Vitae* stresses that "it is a very special form of personal friendship, in which husband and wife generously share everything, without undue reservations or selfish calculations. Whoever truly loves his marriage partner, loves not only for

16

what he receives, but for the partner's self, rejoicing that he can enrich his partner with the gift of himself". The fullness of conjugal love thus understood is connected with its next quality: it is "faithful and exclusive until death. Thus in fact do bride and bridegroom conceive it to be on the day when they freely and in full awareness assume the duty of the marriage bond". And the author of *Humanae Vitae* adds: "A fidelity, this, which can sometimes be difficult, but is always possible (. . .) as no one can deny. (. . .) Not only is fidelity according to the nature of marriage, but it is a source of profound and lasting happiness" (§ 9).

Such a love, proportionate to the exclusive gift between persons to the end of their lives, has the right to be a fruitful love. This is its fourth characteristic, which, as it were, becomes the seal of all its qualities: "This love is fecund, for it is not exhausted by the communion between husband and wife, but is destined to continue, raising up new lives". As we read already in *Gaudium et Spes* § 50 "children are (. . .) the supreme gift of marriage and contribute very substantially to the welfare of their parents".

As we see, the whole image of conjugal love, in which its chief characteristics have emerged and been systematised, points towards fruitfulness, as being the epitome of that interpersonal communion, which *Gaudium et Spes* § 48 defines as the "marriage covenant". Elsewhere *Gaudium et Spes* says that "the spouses, made to the image of the living God and enjoying the authentic dignity of persons (. . .) by the joys and sacrifices of their vocation and through their faithful love (. . .) become witnesses of the mystery of that love which the Lord revealed to the world by his dying and by his rising to life again" (§ 52).

3. *Love and Responsibility*

And thus the encyclical *Humanae Vitae,* referring frequently to the constitution *Gaudium et Spes,* is a special document, giving the teaching of the Church today on the subject of conjugal love. Before approaching the chief theme of this document, namely the problem of responsible parenthood, it is necessary to throw into still greater relief the basic dimension of the responsibility which husband and wife take upon themselves, that is, the responsibility for their love itself.[2] For *this love,* as the specific characteristics listed in *Humanae Vitae* remind us, *is a basic good of marriage,* as it is the basic good of human beings and of mankind. It has been revealed as such by Christ, together with its authentic source in God: "God's love has been poured into our hearts through the Holy Spirit who has been given

18

to us" (Rm 5:5). This good, in which husband and wife participate in a particular and characteristic way, is the basic object of their responsibility. Only those are capable of responsible love in marriage who are imbued with deep responsibility for the gift of love itself. For love is above all a gift, and that is the basic content of its first and continued experience. Although everything seems to confirm that love is a thing "of the world", that it is born in souls and bodies as the fruit of emotional sensitivity and sensuous attraction, reaching to the hidden depths of the sexual constitution of the organism, yet through all this and as if over and above all this, love is a gift. It comes as a gift to those who are in love, allows them to discover and identify each other, then to develop until they reach the suitable point of maturity, and in turn confirm what the Second Vatican Council calls the "marriage covenant", and what is, according to St Paul, a great sacrament in reference to Christ and to the Church (Eph 5:32).

The responsibility for the gift of love finds its expression in an abiding consciousness of having received that gift and at the same time in discerning and appreciating the tasks which accompany the gift. Responsibility for love is not an abstract concept, but is connected with a complex of values, which precisely love allows us to experience in full. These values come to us both as a gift and as a task. A new perspective on life and activity is thus opened and is to lead towards the realisation and fulfilment of these values. If they remain solely a gift, if they do not reach fulfilment, they remain at the stage of a wonderful and fascinating project. Life has to witness to its full reality. Thus responsibility for love becomes responsibility for life, in which definite values find their realisation. In this sense we may say that love engenders responsibility, that love is the special source of responsibility.

The central value, upon which other values in love depend, is the value of the human person. It is to the human person that basic responsibility refers. The texts of the Second Vatican Council affirm many times that love in general, and conjugal love in particular, consists in the gift of one person to another, a gift that embraces the human being as a whole, soul and body. Such a *gift presupposes that the person as such has a unique value for the other person,* which expresses itself in a particular responsibility for that value, precisely because of its degree and because of its intensity, so to speak. And through a responsibility thus conceived there is formed the essential structure of marriage, a bond at once spiritual and moral. This bond embraces and penetrates all that constitutes its psycho-physical wealth and that already issues from the masculinity and femininity of the persons united in wedlock, as their specific psycho-physical endowment. This is connected with a whole scale of manifold values, every one of which enters in its own way into this basic responsibility of husband and wife. Responsibility for love is also responsibility for the person with all that is proper to him or her. *Responsibility for love thus conceived becomes* of itself *the source of development of this love,* both in its main current uniting the two persons indissolubly, and in the various details and situations engendered by the masculine and feminine individualities, with all that is noble and beautiful in them, but also with all that is difficult, contrasting, and sometimes tragic.

As we have mentioned before, the pastoral constitution in its descriptive manner enumerates perhaps more elements which show and explain precisely this dimension of love and responsibility for love:

"The biblical Word of God several times urges the betrothed and the married to nourish and develop their wedlock by pure conjugal love and undivided affection. Many people of our own age also highly regard true love between husband and wife as it manifests itself in a variety of ways, depending on the worthy customs of various peoples and times. This love is an eminently human one since it is directed from one person to another through an affection of the will. It involves the good of the whole person. Therefore it can enrich the expressions of the body and mind with a unique dignity, ennobling these expressions as special ingredients and signs of the friendship distinctive of marriage. This love the Lord has judged worthy of special gifts, healing, perfecting, and exalting gifts of grace and charity. Such love, merging the human with the divine, leads husband and wife to a free and mutual gift of themselves, a gift proving itself by gentle affection and by deed. Such love pervades the whole of their lives. Indeed, by its generous activity it grows better and grows greater. Therefore it far excels mere erotic inclination, which, selfishly pursued, soon enough fades wretchedly away" (§ 49).

4.   *Responsible Parenthood*

It seems that it is impossible to understand the responsible parenthood, of which Paul VI speaks in such a masterly fashion in his encyclical *Humanae Vitae,* in any other way than only by *closely connecting responsible parenthood with responsibility for conjugal love.* As an isolated ethical norm the principle of responsible parenthood is both right and convincing, although in an abstract way. The indispensable lifegiving power, necessary for a principle that should form the life of concrete individuals, flows from love, from responsible

Love, understood and lived in a way which we have tried to sketch above.

And that is why the author of *Humanae Vitae* bases his detailed exposition of responsible parenthood upon the theological character of love, and also upon the premise of the integral vision of man, which becomes fully valid precisely in love and through love. If love signifies this particular responsibility of one person for another person in the reciprocal relation of man and woman, from this responsibility there will also develop, as a matter of course, parenthood in its responsible form.

Parenthood belongs to the nature of this specific love which is conjugal love: it constitutes its essential feature, it forms this love in the sphere of purpose and intention, and signs it finally with the seal of particular fulfilment. *Conjugal love is fulfilled by parenthood.* Responsibility for this love from the beginning to the end is at the same time responsibility also for parenthood. The one participates in the other, and they both constitute each other. Parenthood is a gift that comes to people, to man and to woman, together with love, that creates a perspective of love in the dimension of a reciprocal life-long self-giving, and that is the condition of gradual realisation of that perspective through life and action. Parenthood, the gift, is therefore at the same time a rich task whose receiving and successive fulfilling is synonymous with receiving a gift: a gift, moreover, which the persons themselves become for each other in marriage: the woman for the man, the man for the woman. Their reciprocal offering to each other of what they are as man and woman reaches its full sense through parenthood, through the fact that as husband and wife they become father and mother. And this is precisely the dimension and sense of the responsibility that essentially corresponds to this gift.

". . . While not making the other purposes of matrimony of less account, the true practice of conjugal love and the whole meaning of the family life which results from it, have this aim: that the couple be ready with stout hearts to co-operate with the love of the Creator and the Saviour who through them will enlarge and enrich his own family day by day" (GS § 50).

Thus, following the same logic which is the logic of human conscience and christian faith as well, we *accept the responsibility for parenthood* as one of the elements, or rather *as the constituting element of responsibility for love,* for its conjugal shape and sense. We read further in the pastoral constitution:

"Parents should regard as their proper mission the task of transmitting human life and educating those to whom it has been transmitted. They should realise that they are thereby co-operators with the love of God the Creator, and are, so to speak, the interpreters of that love. Thus they will fulfil their task with human and christian responsibility. With docile reverence towards God, they will come to the right decision by common counsel and effort. They will thoughtfully take into account both their own welfare and that of their children, those already born and those which may be foreseen. For this accounting they will reckon with both the material and spiritual conditions of the times as well as of their state in life. Finally, they will consult the interests of the family group, of temporal society, and of the Church herself. The parents themselves should ultimately make this judgement, in the sight of God" (GS § 50).

In this way, beginning with the concept of responsibility for parenthood — that specific shape and sense that are proper to conjugal love — we approach the concrete problem which is given the name of "responsible parenthood". It is indispensable, both for the theoretical considerations of science and teaching and also for the practical application, to *preserve in this matter a consistent point of view,* for only such consistency permits us to understand rightly, to pose and to resolve the problem. It is a matter of consistency of perspective and of plan as well: responsibility for parenthood is engendered through conjugal love, understood and experienced in a responsible way, that is, according to all its interior truth, in the fullness of the sense and meaning of that love. Thus understood and experienced, responsibility for parenthood allows the husband and wife to pose the problem of responsible parenthood correctly in their thinking, their appraisal and their judgement, and also to *solve that problem correctly* in their life and concrete behaviour. If this correctness reaches the sphere of the so-called methods of birth control, even here the husband and wife will not forego what constitutes the authentic measure of responsibility for love, and therefore both the essential value of the person, and the dignity of parenthood connected with it. Speaking more plainly: they will not have recourse to contraception, which is essentially opposed to love and parenthood.[3]

This is the aim and the demand of the Church as set forth in the encyclical *Humanae Vitae,* while in the pastoral constitution we read as follows: "In their manner of acting spouses should be aware that they cannot proceed arbitrarily. They must always be governed according to a conscience dutifully conformed to the divine law itself, and should be submissive towards the Church's teaching office, which authentically interprets that law in the light of the Gospel. That divine law reveals and protects the integral meaning of conjugal love, and impels it towards a truly human fulfilment" (GS § 50).

5. An Upright Conscience

The contemporary teaching of the Church about responsible parenthood refers, as we see, to the divine law, to the authentic sense of conjugal love, to the integral vision of man. Through all this it endeavours to appeal to the conscience of man, to that point in which everything finally converges, and from which issue judgements upon action, and even actions themselves in their conscious and voluntary shape. The pivot of the whole matter is the *conscience*. It is self-evident that in all other fields of human morality conscience is also in the final analysis the decisive factor, and the value of human deeds depends upon it directly, but *in this chapter of morality conscience becomes the crucial point in a particular fashion*. We are here in the sphere of a type of action and co-operation, in which two people, a man and a woman, remain totally alone with each other, thrown upon what they are, not only in their physical masculinity and femininity, but also in their interior experiencing of each other, in that experience which of its nature is of an intimate character, hidden from the world and from the judgement of others. In such a situation one's own conscience seems particularly decisive: an upright and mature conscience, a conscience both human and christian will indicate here and now the proper measure of responsibility. "The parents themselves should ultimately make this judgement, in the sight of God", we read in *Gaudium et Spes* § 50. Responsibility for love and responsibility for parenthood may finally be reduced to the many judgements of conscience of the husband and wife, to the decisions in which a whole scale of values is correctly or wrongly voiced, and also to a whole scale of duties, contained in each such act. Each act of this kind reveals it and verifies it, fortifies or weakens it, founds or destroys it.

And that is why *everything* contained in the constitution *Gaudium et Spes,* in the encyclical *Humanae Vitae,* and in their wake in a whole series of other pronouncements: pastoral letters, instructions, exhortations, and further still in publications, books, pamphlets, in courses, conferences and lectures — everything contained in them and transmitting the teaching of the Church[4] *is finally aimed at forming an upright and mature conscience in husband and wife.*

The meaning of parenthood, and in particular of responsible parenthood , is above all ethical. Human conscience is at its centre. At its centre is man, with the grave authority of his conscience and of the value attached to it, which basically determines him. We must endeavour to do all that is possible not to allow the deep ethical sense of responsible parenthood to become alienated. The encyclical *Humanae Vitae* (after the constitution *Gaudium et Spes*) repeats many times that parenthood belongs, so to speak, to the substance of conjugal love. True conjugal love possesses the characteristic and privilege of fertility. The Church renders justice, through the words of the Pope and of the Council, to those married couples who generously accept the responsibility for numerous children. The Church however takes under consideration various conditions and circumstances: "If, then, there are serious motives to space out births, which derive from the physical or psychological conditions of husband and wife, or from external conditions, the Church teaches that it is then licit to take into account the natural rhythms immanent in the generative functions, for the use of marriage in the infecund periods only, and in this way to regulate birth without offending the moral principles which have been recalled earlier" (HV § 16).

The meaning, attributed to responsible parenthood by Paul VI, in accordance with the Second Vatican Council and the whole tradition of christian teaching of faith and morality, *is essentially ethical.* In virtue of this, and with great insistence, Paul VI strictly distinguishes between this form of "birth control" which the Church can recognise as compatible with the divine law, and that which is commonly called "contraception", and what in the pontifical document is defined as "artificial birth control". In the first case the husband and wife avail themselves in a correct fashion of a certain peculiar property given to them by nature; in the second, they obstruct the natural course of processes, connected with the transmission of life. It is true nonetheless, that in both cases husband and wife, by mutual and explicit consent, wish to avoid the transmission of life and want to be sure that a child will not be conceived. "It is true that in the one and the other case the married couple are concordant in the positive will of avoiding children for plausible reasons, seeking the certainty that offspring will not arrive; but it is also true that in the former case only are they able to renounce the use of marriage in fecund periods when, for just motives, procreation is not desirable while making use of it during infecund periods to manifest their affection and to safeguard their mutual fidelity. By so doing, they give proof of a truly and integrally honest love" (HV § 16).

The author of the encyclical is conscious of the psychological difficulties, and perhaps even intellectual ones which the standpoint of the Church may meet. That is why those who take up this standpoint *must have a clear understanding* not only of the decisions themselves but of all the reasons on which these decisions are based. In practice especially they must not allow the morality of the action to be confused with the technique of the action, the principle to be confused with the method. One of the fundamental errors in the interpretation of *Humanae Vitae* proceeds precisely from this confusion. The modern "technical" mentality wants to see above all a "technique" (and manipulation) also in the case where two people, a man and a woman, as husband and wife, *must face each other in the whole truth of their mutual gift, guided by their upright and mature conscience.* The Church wants to save the true sense of love for them, and the mature dignity of behaviour proper to persons. That is also the true reason of continence, which constitutes an indispensable condition not only of responsible parenthood, but also of responsibility for conjugal love itself.[5]

One of the essential factors of this love, whose irreplaceable teacher is Christ himself, is the capacity of exacting and accepting such demands, without which love could not be itself. The concern for such an authentic shape of human love has dictated also these requirements, which Paul VI has formulated in the encyclical *Humanae Vitae* in accordance with the tradition of Catholic teaching. Do we not feel this concern, for instance, in the following fragment?

"It is (. . .) to be feared that the man, growing used to the employment of anti-conceptive practices, may finally lose respect for the woman and, no longer caring for her physical and psychological equilibrium, may come to the point of considering her as a mere instrument of selfish enjoyment, and no longer as his respected and beloved companion" (HV § 17).

6. *A Common Concern*

We all, present here today, have gathered in the name of the same concern which has dictated to the Fathers of the Second Vatican Council their words on the promotion of the dignity of marriage and the family, and to Paul VI the encyclical *Humanae Vitae,* while paying no regard to the voices of protest and opposition, easily foreseen. On this tenth anniversary of the appearance of that document, re-reading it in the context of the constitution *Gaudium et Spes,* we find the following words, which seem singularly pertinent: "Redeeming the present time, and distinguishing eternal realities from their changing expressions, Christians should actively promote the values of marriage and the family, both by the example of their own lives and by co-operation

with other men of good will. Thus when difficulties arise, Christians will provide, on behalf
of family life, those necessities and helps which
are suitably modern. To this end, the christian
instincts of the faithful, the upright moral con-
sciences of men, and the wisdom and experience of persons versed in the sacred sciences
will have much to contribute" (GS § 52).

The cause which has called us together is
worthy of common concern, and also worthy
of our highest effort and engagement. Marriage
and the family are invariably at the root of all
the affairs of man and society. *Although in
itself it is,* one might say, a most *private concern,* an affair of two persons, of husband and
wife, and of the smallest social group, which
they form together with their children, yet *the
fate of nations and continents, of humanity
and of the Church depends upon it.* Probably
among the persons present here there are some
for whom the problem of an ethical birth
control is important because of a high birth
rate in their country; but there are also those
who, quite to the contrary, are worried by the
process of a declining or demographical
endangering of their own nation. It is self-
evident that the great political and economical
processes possess their true foundation, both
their starting point and their goal, in every
married couple and in every family. If the
Second Vatican Council stresses the need of

fostering their dignity, it points thus to the basic method and direction of solutions in this field. This method and direction must not be first of all quantitative, but essentially qualitative, for these matters are very deeply inserted into the meaning of human life: they speak of the very value of man and also constitute it.

All this is and should be the *object of great concern,* and of *concern in common.* In the name of this concern we have gathered here. May the Holy Spirit, the Spirit of Jesus Christ, through the intercession of his Mother, the spiritual Mother of all people, accompany our discussion. May our meeting, the meeting of people of good will, of the best will, participate in that "christian sense", and in that "upright conscience", that "wisdom and experience" of which the Council document speaks.

These gifts of the Holy Spirit, these attributes of the intellect, of the will and of the heart are indispensable in this work, whose aim is "fostering the dignity of marriage and of the family".

NOTES

[1] Cf. *Humanae Vitae* § 23ff. See also *Gaudium et Spes* § 2.

[2] The author of this lecture has developed these problems in his work: K. Wojtyla, *Milosc i odpowiedzialnosc. Studium etyczne*, Kraków, Znak 1962; Italian translation: *Amore e responsabilità*, Roma, Marietti 1968.

[3] P. Chauchard, *Amour et contraception*, Mame 1967. Under the same title Chauchard delivered a lecture during the session on "Specialistic Aspects of the Problem of Contraception", organised by the Family Institute of the Pontifical Faculty of Theology in Kraków on February 7-8, 1976.

[4] Cf., e.g., the comments on *Humanae Vitae*, published in *Notificationes* 1-4 (1969) edited by the Metropolitan Curia of Kraków; Italian translation: "Introduzione all'enciclica *Humanae Vitae*" da 'Notificationes' e Curia Metropolitana Cracoviensi A.D. 1969, Januaris-Aprilis N. 1-4.

See also the letter of the Episcopate of Poland addressed to priests on preparing the faithful for the Sacrament of Marriage and on pastoral theology of the family, February 12, 1969.

[5] Cf. *Humanae Vitae* § 9, 10; also *Gaudium et Spes* § 50.

35

FRUITFUL AND RESPONSIBLE LOVE

Comments and Reactions

If judgement on the person of Karol Wojtyla as Pope has to await the perspective of history, we have sufficient knowledge already of the person of the Archbishop of Cracow, the scholar and pastor.

The contribution he has given over at least the past ten years to the pontifical commission for the study of population and to the committee for the family of the *Consilium de laicis* — to mention but two areas that specifically regard the family — has been important enough to testify to a lively and vigilant awareness of the problems that the family faces.

This awareness is no mere happening of chance. The particular situation in which the Church in Poland is set necessarily focuses attention on the family. In a context where the other institutions of education are almost monopolised by the State (in the best of hypotheses lay, in the worst the bearer of an openly atheistic ideology) the family assumes a determining role for the very continuity of the Church and for the carrying through of its mission of evangelisation.

The overall view on which the Cracovian Cardinal's address to the C.I.S.F. Congress was based undoubtedly took this context into consideration. But the greatest merit of the address was manifested by a lively and at the same time open fidelity to the Council's message. The great texts of *Gaudium et Spes* on marriage and the family, and not only the indications of the encyclical *Humanae Vitae,* were at the centre of that address anticipating to some degree — if one takes into consideration the opening message of John Paul II — what will be the main thrust of his pontificate, that is, a constant referral to Vatican II and to its teaching.

In this profound — and not simply lexical — fidelity to the Council there are to be found as well, in our opinion, the innovating possibilities incapsulated in that address of June 1978. In an "open" and "pastoral" reading of the Council there is necessarily included the constant referral to the married couple, to their difficulties, to their situation in the concrete. Here are in play the values of christian life not on a doctrinal level but on the existential level and it is here that the destiny of the family — for that matter the destiny of the Church — is determined.

Actually it is in this context, precisely because of his pastoral sensitivity, that John Paul II could turn out to be a cautious innovator. And in the Church the most profound innovations, the ones that give the most abundant fruit, are precisely those that go hand in hand with fidelity to tradition.

Giorgio Campanini lectures in family sociology at the University of Parma and is a member of the Scientific Committee of C.I.S.F. (Italy).

41

Ever since Cardinal Wojtyla was elected Pope I have lived on one tiny story. It is my habit when I attend a conference to take brief notes of what speakers say and then to make a rapid evaluation of the significance of their contribution with some sign which signifies outstanding value. When I brought my notes home after the Milan conference I noted that only one speaker had a star against his name and that was Cardinal Wojtyla. I now treasure the notes, the star, and show them off to my friends.

The reader may want to know why I accorded such an accolade to the Cardinal's address. My first and predominant reason was that the contents of his address were principally concerned with love in marriage, and I believe that the world is hungry for a deeper appreciation of the meaning of love in marriage and the family. My second reason was that the bulk of the address was concerned with love between persons, the spouses, and the spouses' children, and this is precisely the great step forward of Vatican II of conceiving marriage and the family as a community of love. Thirdly, because the address finished by being preoccupied with the central task of the Church, namely, the dignity of marriage and the family. On the whole there was very little about birth control and contraception, and a great deal about love, person, and the responsibility of love between people. I feel that this is precisely the order of priority in the tasks facing the Church today, and intuitively the speaker had got the order of values right. In other words, the problems facing the Church in contraception have to be subordinated to the infinitely greater task of showing the world the meaning of christian love in the marital and parental encounter, for it is this love that brings the true reality of Christ to the very heart of this sacrament.

Nevertheless, the teaching of *Humanae Vitae* remains divisive inside the Church. The Cardinal refers to the encyclical's psychological and intellectual difficulties and I interpreted his address as saying that only by concentrating on understanding the gift of personal love between spouses and spouses and their children are we likely to reconcile the divisions over contraception. And so the challenge remains continuously in an ever-deepening understanding of love in contemporary marriage.

Contemporary marriage brings men and women together who relate on a much more intimate, egalitarian relationship than in the past. In the West where there has been a rise in material standards there is imperceptibly a

44

seeking of fulfilment of love at deeper personal layer of social and psychological significance. At the latter level there is a longing for greater realisation of love expressed in feelings, emotions and instincts.

This deeper yearning is seeking sustaining, healing and growth. As far as sustaining is concerned, the couple look towards each other for material sustaining and the much greater employment of women nowadays means that there is a mutual sharing of economic responsibility. But beyond material sustaining couples expect to be supported emotionally. They expect to feel secure in each other's presence and to receive the constant affirmation that will make them feel recognised, wanted and appreciated. There is a deeper layer of their personhood which calls for acknowledgment of each other. In the past provided the spouses dutifully acted their respective roles of: (a) husband — head of the family and main economic support and (b) mother — childbearer and rearer and house-keeper, then it was considered that they ful-filled their duty. Now couples expect to go beyond these roles which are exchangeable (apart from childbearing) and sometimes roles can be reversed, to the depths of their being where they want to be understood, reached and acknowledged.

Beyond sustaining they are also expecting to be healed. Spouses come to each other at the beginning of marriage with a variety of wounds and these wounds come from the personality which may be moody, overanxious, prone to impulsive anger, fearful, lacking in confidence or self-esteem or excessively self-critical, feeling unloveable. These are the ravages of heredity and upbringing and the spouse becomes a channel of grace through which healing can occur. Through acceptance, affirmation, encouragement, presentation of alternative views of their worth wounded men and women can be healed and this is one of the precious features of the intimate encounter of love in marriage.

Finally, spouses may live with each other for some fifty years of marriage. During these years they change and grow in maturity. It may be the maturity of the body, which converts physical gifts to athletic achievement, or intellect which is converted to wisdom, or caring into a penetrating and ever-widening capacity to love. The couple stand as the principal source of encouragement, mutual support and help for this growth.

Vatican II speaks of special gifts which the Lord gives to the married, gifts of healing and perfecting. It is the task of social scientists to penetrate into the mystery of marital love and unravel the form this love takes in contemporary marriages which are in such a period of transition. Love between spouses in these circumstances is giving and enriching the life of each other, preparing the spouses for the moment when their mutuality can give rise to new life.

Sexual intercourse has a variety of meaning in this loving encounter between the spouses. It is primarily a body language of love which reinforces the sustaining, healing and growth of the couple. But each sexual act has its own potential existential meaning. The language of the body, expressed through pleasure and delight, can say, with or without words, "Thank you" to each other. It is the means of expressing gratitude for the presence and availability of each other. It has the means of expressing hope for the future, namely, that the spouses will stay together and grow in love. It is the means through which conflicts can be reconciled and thus intercourse becomes a means of forgiveness. It is the means through which the sexual identity of the couple can recurrently be affirmed. It is finally the means through which the personhood of each other can be repeatedly validated. The erotic, which God the creator gave man as a precious gift, becomes one of the most powerful and economic languages of love, giving life to the spouses as persons.

Those who have difficulties with the biological openness to life in every sexual act see every act of coitus as life-giving in these personal terms which desire any means of achievement. There is a strong case to be made for such an argument. But there are also difficulties of a different type than those mentioned in the encyclical. There are mechanical forms of contraception which diminish the physical contact of the personal encounter and thus reduce the integrity of the exchange. Sheaths, caps, coitus interruptus, all have these disadvantages. The pill does not have this disadvantage but nevertheless by eliminating ovulation, it reduces the physical pressure of the means of transmitting life and thus the integrity of the person.

Is there a way of reconciling the views of those who oppose *Humanae Vitae* on the grounds that there is no essential connection between every act of coitus and new life and those who feel that what matters is the free flow of love between people? The latter claim that the existential significance of coitus is its supreme value and the biological must be subordinated to it. The adherents of *Humanae Vitae* may agree on the supreme value of love in personal encounter but not at the price of eliminating the biological connection with life. The point of reconciliation may be the agreement that the personal encounter of love between people as husband and wife is the supreme value. That while contraception may be used to achieve this in special circumstances each contraceptive should be judged on its merits in allowing a full physical and emotional encounter, the least desirable contraceptive being those that detract most seriously from the integrity of the personal encounter. But the ultimate integrity of the encounter is respect for the whole person, body, mind, feelings and soul. It is this ideal that should be aimed for as the christian one. It is an ideal to be presented to christian couples who are asked to work towards it by degrees and ultimately including continence, not as a denial of the value of coitus but as a sacrifice towards the ideal of the integrity of the encounter of the whole person which respects their totality. A growth towards an ideal love rather than an absolute prohibition may be the point of reconciliation.

Whatever the resolution on contraception, clearly coitus serves the life of spouses as persons who in turn give new life and nurture it with love, a supreme challenge of creativity. Coitus now becomes the means of raising new life and sustaining it by its contribution to the life of the parents.

Thus the dignity of marriage is to be found in the series of relationships of love, first between the spouses which require permanency and faithfulness to nourish them in a monogamous and exclusive relationship, in the relationship of love between the parents and their children which requires responsible nurturing for their mature development, finally the openness of the whole family to the community in which other people become our neighbour, the Christ we respond to by loving them to the fullness of our strength.

Dr. J. Dominian, well-known author, is consultant psychiatrist at Central Middlesex Hospital, London.

François and Michele Guy

On the evening of October 16, 1978, the out-come of the Conclave took us back four months to the C.I.S.F. Congress at Milan where Cardinal Karol Wojtyla delivered the opening address.

His talk, entitled "Fruitful and Responsible Love", was the theme of the five-day inter-national meeting where the representatives of fifty-seven countries, invited by Fr Charles Vella, had assembled.

Looking back through our notes we see the lucid cogency with which the Cardinal spoke on *Humanae Vitae,* on Marriage, on Love. We remembered, particularly, what he had insistently pointed out, i.e., the encyclical was not an isolated act of the pontificate of Pope Paul VI. It could be traced in a direct line to Vatican II, more specifically to the constitution *Gaudium et Spes,* an expression, consequently, of the conviction of all the Council Fathers.

We admired the logic of his reasoning, the exactness of his quotations, and the way in which he showed how fecundity is inseparably linked to the dynamic of Human Love; that no one of these characteristics — totality, fidelity, exclusiveness, fecundity — can be brushed aside. Each one of us was also invited to rediscover, in a free and responsible manner, the inseparable bond between respect for life and the richness of love!

This is, above all, what we have remembered of his thinking. And of the man? We looked again at the photographs we brought with us. They bring to mind the vivid picture we have kept of him, the expression of a smiling yet reserved serenity, a boundless sense of welcome, full of kindness yet tinged with modesty and prudence.

Overall, we experienced the impression of a quite exceptional "presence", of power, of resolute strength . . . or quite simply perhaps, one of those Rocks, one of those Stones on which (we know this today) the Church is set.

Drs. François and *Michele Guy* are co-directors of I.R.E.C. (Institut Recherche Enfant et Couple). Dr. François Guy is also Vice-President of I.F.F.L.P. (France).

My first meeting with the then Cardinal Wojtyla was last April. The Scientific Committee of C.I.S.F., of which I am a member, had resolved some months before to ask the Cardinal — whose sensitivity to family problems was well known to us — to explain in his introductory address the Church's position on this problem in its historical, theological, and pastoral perspective.

Our request was sent by letter and Cardinal Wojtyla accepted immediately. In March, however, when I informed Fr Charles Vella, the Director of C.I.S.F., that I would have to spend two weeks at Cracow in a professional capacity, we agreed that it would be a most opportune occasion to express personally the organising committee's gratitude. As well, an elucidation of the aims and the programme of the Congress would facilitate his task.

I can recall the easy-going way the Cardinal received me at his residence and the warmth of his welcome which quickly dissipated my understandable initial uneasiness; the lively interest he showed when, in a long and cordial talk, he wanted to be informed in detail on the themes and the aims of the Congress; the profound sense of sharing when dealing with the problems of married people and the family. But what struck me, most of all, was the profound ecumenical meaning, awareness, and worry that shone through from his words regarding the objective difficulties of getting the christian message down into the local and contingent situations where those involved in the pastoral ministry and family consultants worked.

And in his opening address, which we heard two months later at Milan in all its doctrinal exactness, afforded all those who were present a sure reference point which allowed the work sessions to preserve an ideal unity, to which the witness of the Catholic and non-Catholic participants from every part of the globe constructively related their characteristics, thus contributing largely to the success of the Congress.

Vincenzo Lorenzelli lectures at the University of Genoa and is President of the Promoter Group of christian inspired Family Consultants.

The majority of people in the Church and even in the world was stunned with happiness at the election of John Paul II as Pope. After the ray of light — the appearance of John Paul I — it is as if the promise that was this Pope of one morning had been recaptured all over again and this time held fast. Supreme roguishness of the Spirit and his servants that this concatenation of choice and surprise which led, in turn, to the most unexpected and yet most necessary renewal! One could say that without Pope John XXIII, Paul VI would have been a Pius XIII. It was the wish of John Paul I to be the synthesis of "John" and "Paul". It is to his successor, just as unexpected as he was, that this task will fall as he brings to the chair of the head of the Apostles what Slavonic genius holds most precious in its Catholic and Roman fidelity.

With John Paul II it is also the Church of silence, the Church of poverty that takes up the word and the helm to serve Christ in the Church of Peter. So, for the second time, humanly speaking, the fisherman's barque passes into the hands of a worker's son. But what is more, for the first time in our days, it passes into the hands of a son of one of those Churches recently dispossessed in the temporal sphere and become a Church of confession beyond all others. Who will say that we, above all in the West, no longer need to thrill again with holy joy on hearing this new voice recall our greatness and our duty as Christians?

As for the *International Centre for the Study of Family Life* it can quite rightly see a singular sign of encouragement in the fact that John Paul II came as Cardinal Wojtyla at its last Congress. As for me it goes without saying that if I had guessed that Cardinal Wojtyla was going to be the future Pope, I would never have taken the floor in front of him at the Congress in the first place! On the other hand, everyone else — except the man himself — would have stopped me! Nonetheless, one thing is surely more certain. His service as Pope at Rome will bear the same characteristics as his contribution at Milan: an absolute fidelity to the Council and to the whole of the Council. This was already the line of Paul VI under his leadership and in his teaching. Now in such men as these we know what fidelity means. Consequently, John Paul II will not be a Pope who will ever step back when faced with the difficult problems that were tackled at the Milan Congress and in this line he will be a unique light for the Centre.

Praise then to the Lord for the gift that he has given us of such a Pope and a sense of security also for those persons who work unreservedly and fearlessly in the sensitive areas of faith and morals.

Gustave Martelet is a member of the International Theological Commission (France).

We wish to express our joy at the election of Cardinal Wojtyla of Poland as Supreme Pontiff and Pope John Paul II. In electing a person from outside Italy as Pope, we are reminded of the universality of the Church and its central administration for the Vatican. In electing a man from Poland, the guiding light of the Holy Spirit is felt in having at the head of the Catholic Church a man who is sensitive to the suffering of people and who, besides having been confined himself by occupation forces, has been bold in fighting for the cause of liberation of his people from oppression.

Only last June 1978 at the international Congress organised by the C.I.S.F. at Milan, I had the privilege of meeting often Pope John Paul II (then Cardinal Wojtyla) and discussing with him various issues regarding family life. In his address on the opening session of that Congress, he emphasised the concern of the Catholic Church for those families who were striving hard to live their christian values. He stressed the depth of responsibility to which a couple is called upon in the realisation of these values and the genuine points of conflict that a couple is faced with in all sincerity and loyalty to the teaching of the Church. He called upon all Family Life Workers to make available to these couples the fruit of their learning and research in the Natural Methods of Family Planning. He also asked Pastors and Family Life Workers to develop a deep sense of love and concern for the families troubled by this responsibility and, without any condemnation, to extend to them at all times a hand of support and friendship and thus help them to overcome their hurdles.

It was particularly a joyful experience to discuss with His Holiness about the various facets of family life, as applied to Third World countries like India. He showed great interest in the Family Pastoral Service offered by the Indian Episcopal Commission on Family and its National Family Secretariat. He was quite interested to know of the tremendous progress made in the field of Natural Family Planning in India, through the various Regional Family Centres and also of the supportive educational and enrichment programmes like Family Life Education, Marriage Preparation, Family Movements, etc.

I was always struck with the simplicity of the man, mixing freely with the delegates and genuinely concerned in coming to know more about their work. It is obvious that this arises from his deep sense of commitment to the

Family Apostolate as the mainstay of the progress of the Church. Already in the sessions of Vatican II, we had occasion to sense his grip of the situation, when he emphasised the necessity for harmonious marital relations and went on to expound the various facets that go to strengthen these relations and the possible weak points which have to be strengthened.

In greeting His Holines Pope John Paul II into his position, we who are workers in the Family Pastoral Services in India, have a special feeling of closeness for one who has placed "family values" in high priority for the strengthening of the Church in the future. We look up to him for concern and guidance for the many families, especially in the developing countries, who are faced with grave problems every day of their lives (which is more of an existence) and who yet have the joy of simplicity, sincerity and faith for the love of God for his people.

Dr. A. F. A. Mascarenhas, M.S., F.R.C.S., is professor of surgery, St John's Medical College and National Secretary of the C.B.C.I. Commission for Family and Laity.

A meeting with any human being is always an historical event. This truth was brought home to me at Milan on June 21, 1978, on the occasion of the international Congress on "Fruitful and Responsible Love".

The man who has become the spiritual head of the Roman Catholic Church had spent some ten or so minutes with me, before his opening address, in which we made a survey of questions concerning the family which interested our Churches.

In this talk and in his address of the following points certain traits of Cardinal Karol Wojtyla became apparent to me:

First, he is a noble-minded man, open towards the other Churches which are made up not of separated brethren, but of Christians who bring other spiritual dimensions to Christianity.

Secondly, he is openly sympathetic and warm-hearted towards people of other cultures and races.

Thirdly, he is a man whose countenance characterises a sense of reconciliatory dialogue, a man ever ready to serve as intermediary between persons and countries whose ways of thinking and political and economic outlook are even contradictory.

Fourthly, although marked by the tradition of the Church, he is a man who is free because he believes in the reformatory strength of the divine Spirit.

His commentary on *Humanae Vitae* was made not from the standpoint of a philosopher or a biologist but of a pastor participating in the joy and anguish of husband and wife. He reminded them of the divine and uncalculating character of fruitful love; this love that is ongoing, which transmits life not simply to pro- duce new lives but because it creates fruitful interaction between two persons in an indis- solubly sanctified relationship. He reminded the Church as well, that love is an act of free will uniting man and woman. It is in this free union that husband and wife learn to safeguard human values.

While opposed to contraception, Cardinal Wojtyla accepts, however, the reality of the couple's freedom of conscience in the process of responsible parenthood and of regulating birth. There is the discovery of tradition and the enrichment of pastoral care towards people in their particular situations.

We hope that the new Pope will continue to

address himself to married couples and will allow ecumenical meetings and dialogue in order to get to the bottom of the question of fruitful and responsible love. For to this is tied the problem of the regulation of birth which cries out for new theological and pastoral insights.

ma Mpolo Masamba, former Dean of the Protestant Faculty of Theology (Zaire) and Executive Secretary and Project Director Office of Family Education of the World Council of Churches (Switzerland).

Giacomo Perico

The opening address of the then Cardinal Wojtyla at the international Congress on the theme "Fruitful and Responsible Love" signalled, in my opinion, not only the *point of major equilibration* within the area of the impressive and serene comparison of positions and ideas which emerged from the Congress but also marked *a convincing way of approaching the encyclical.* Ten years after its promulgation, *Humanae Vitae* faces the world without losing any of its credibility; indeed, it is enriched with a broad range of experience "which speaks in favour of the truth of the doctrine contained in the encyclical and of its essential soundness".

The most intense and specific aspect of Cardinal Wojtyla's talk is marked by this lively sense of principles as well as by a pastoral sense of the reality of human existence which, in so vast a problem, is profoundly disturbed. In fact, the speaker said, on the one hand, the authentic vision of love leads husband and wife necessarily to a programme of responsible parenthood while calling to mind those elements that could impose avoiding children. On the other hand, the typical value of the person and the most noble characteristics of the person's fatherhood and motherhood — in their turn closely linked to the view of a plan and gesture of love — do not allow recourse to contraceptive means which contradict such values. In this overall and absolutely specific vision of man, the ideal and consistent way when faced with the problem of responsible procreation is renouncing "contraception which is essentially opposed to love and parenthood". This, said the speaker, is the goal "that protects the integral meaning of conjugal love and impels it towards a truly human fulfilment" (*Gaudium et Spes,* n. 50).

The ideal goal towards which the believing couple is called by dint of reason and faith passes, in the ultimate analysis, through the voice of conscience where all laws in some way converge and from which issue the indications and the concrete judgements of the operative choices in their conscious and free form. Thus conscience constitutes "the crucial point of the problem" of responsible parenthood insofar as it is in its competence to determine the choice of the action which is to be effectuated in a direct and immediate manner.

To this must be added, as well, that in the specific problem of parenthood — since we are looking at an action "in which a man and a woman remain totally alone with each other, thrown upon what they are, not only in their physical masculinity and feminity, but also in their interior experiencing of each other, in that experience which of its nature is of an intimate character, hidden from the world and from the judgement of others" — their conscience fulfils a particularly decisive role.

It goes without saying that for this conscience to be in a position to fulfil the operative indication in the specific problem of parenthood it must be duly *enlightened* by suitable means of information among which, at least for the believer, there must certainly be enumerated the indications of the Magisterium. Further, this conscience must be *upright,* that is, willing to seek out truth wherever it thinks it can be found. Finally, conscience must be *mature,* that is, disposed to stimulating the fulfilment of what it retains "must be done". In a word, summed up the speaker, conscience must be "both human and christian".

It was along this great guiding line of an upright, mature, human and christian conscience, outlined by the Archbishop of Cracow, that the Congress was able to lead the participants back to a *more careful and comprehensive reading of the encyclical* in its most profound aspects, in its pastoral application, yet all the while respecting the principles that rule human action.

Summing up, along the lines of this basic outline, we could say that there emerged from the Congress a sufficiently clear-cut directive of this type: *For those who had the privilege* of understanding the true and profound sense of love, it appears clear that, in the wake of the encyclical *Humanae Vitae,* there exists ample room in which to develop one's own gift of love, even that of the joy of sacrifice.

For those who have not had this privilege there must be, on the part of the pastor, a lively sense of charity which respects their still insufficiently enlightened and mature conscience. Such being the case, the norms of the encyclical — while being for them a great light towards which they strive wholeheartedly — can still turn out to be quite difficult. These norms, therefore, are to be propounded with good grace, *in a way that the pontifical document does not appear as the "enemy" of man* and grieved over his existence, but a pointer towards life and perfection. We cannot ask people who are not athletes to scale steep mountains. Good sense, in these cases, requires above all, moving slowly.

The upshot of this is not to distort *Humanae Vitae* but to *revalue it.* The encyclical is still a reference point, a distant point of arrival, even if the effort to follow the rules brings with it delusion, deflection and difficulties.

"To omit nothing of the saving doctrine of Christ is an eminent form of charity towards souls. But this must always be accompanied by the patience and goodness of which the Lord gave an example in his dealing with people. He who came not to judge but to save was most certainly intransigent with evil, but merciful towards the sinner" (*Humanae Vitae*, n. 29).

Giacomo Perico is a moral theologian and a specialist in family problems. He was formerly a member of the pontifical commission for the study of population, family and genetics.

When, in the evening of October 16, I heard the announcement that Karol Wojtyla was the new bishop of Rome and Pope of the universal Church, an immense joy filled my heart and I thought immediately of the Milan Congress where, the previous June 21 and 22 we both gave a talk on the doctrine of marriage.

I recalled with gratitude the evening meal and the breakfast we had taken together. He conveyed to me his loving and vigilant care for the seminarians of his diocese and he invited me to come and speak one day at Cracow.

On Sunday, October 22, after the marvellous eucharistic celebration in St Peter's Square, he received the ecumenical delegation and I had the joy of meeting him personally. He embraced me and his first words were to recall our association at the Milan Congress and his joy that I had been so close to him in the expression of the common faith concerning christian marriage. He expressed his hope that the scandal of division would come to an end, and I think that his pontificate will see a reconstitution of the visible unity of all Christians.

Standing there, face to face with Pope John Paul II, I felt a sense of renewal in my commitment to do all in my power so that we could joyfully be reunited in the fullness of faith and the Eucharist.

I recall the talk he gave at Milan (June 21): the depth of his faith, the clarity of his teaching, the fervour of his piety and, at the same time, his openness and understanding of all the problems of married people and the family.

He is the Pope of the Council's accomplishment, the Pope of *Lumen Gentium* and of *Gaudium et Spes,* the Pope of the word of God and of the living liturgy. I feel sure that with him the Church is going to take cognizance of a renewal of faith in the openness and fidelity of the great tradition.

Max Thurian is a Calvinist theologian and Vicar Prior of the Community of Taizé (France).